THE STARS' TRIP TO EARTH

Dedicated to our eighth-grade English teacher, Leslie Linda Mesman, for her enthusiasm toward our ideas and for her wonderful support

Published by Willowisp Press, Inc.
801 94th Avenue North, St. Petersburg, Florida 33702

Copyright © 1993 by Willowisp Press, Inc.

All rights reserved. No portion of this book may be reproduced, stored in a retrieval system, or transmitted, in any form or by any means, electronic, mechanical, photocopying, recording, or otherwise without prior written permission from the publisher.

Printed in the United States of America

2 4 6 8 10 9 7 5 3 1

ISBN 0-87406-650-6

THE STARS' TRIP TO EARTH

Written and illustrated by eighth-grade students at Ecole Viscount Alexander, Winnipeg, Manitoba: Morag Crawford, Lise Brown, and Jennifer Oakes.

Coordinated by Teacher Leslie Mesman and Librarian Mona-Lynne Howden. School Principal is Claire Painchaud.

One day a group of stars wanted to go on a trip, but where?

They had already gone to the moon, Mars, Venus—even the sun. Where could they go now?

"To the earth," a little star yelled.

"Why, that's a good idea. It would be fun. Come on, guys, we're going to the earth."

The next day they left. They all piled into the tiny starship. Then off they went.

But one star fell through the clouds. He fell

        down,

              down,

                    down to the earth.

He was the very first falling star!

When they reached earth, they all went different ways.

One star went to the ocean. He liked it there, and he stayed.

He was the first starfish!

Another star went to the forest. He liked all the animals and the trees. But when he began to get sleepy, he climbed to the top of a tall, tall spruce tree. He liked it there, and he stayed.

He was the first Christmas tree star!

Another star fell into a jar. He made it his home.

Everyone loved the jar because at night it glowed. The star liked it there, and he stayed.

He was the first light bulb!

The clumsy star, his name was Ed. He fell into a well. He couldn't get out. He didn't mind, because he was a wishing star. He liked it there.

He was the first wishing well!

But the little star was now all alone. He wanted to go home. He was homesick.

He jumped and jumped until he shot up into the sky.

He was the first shooting star!

Just think, if the stars had never gone on their trip to earth, the world would not be the same.

Kids Are Authors™ Award Information

The SBF Teacher Support Foundation, formerly known as the SBF J. Hilbert Sapp Foundation, established the Kids Are Authors™ Competition to recognize young authors and illustrators, and to encourage them to continue in their creative endeavors.

The Kids Are Authors™ Competition is a book-writing contest for groups of students from the United States and Canada. Entries are judged by a panel of professionals from the field of children's literature, and each year the winning book is published.

For more information on the Kids Are Authors™ Competition write to:

In Canada,

Great Owl Book Fairs, Inc.
Kids Are Authors™ Competition
257 Finchdene Square, Unit 7
Scarborough, Ontario M1X 1B9

In the U.S.A.,

SBF Services, Inc.
Kids Are Authors™ Competition
801 94th Avenue North
St. Petersburg, Florida 33702

Winners in the annual Kids Are Authors™ Competition

1992: *The Stars' Trip to Earth* (Canadian winner) by eighth graders of Ecole Viscount Alexander, Winnipeg, Manitoba.
How the Sun Was Born (U.S. winner) by third graders of Drexel Elementary School, Tucson, Arizona.

1991: *My Principal Lives Next Door!* by third graders of Sanibel Elementary School, Sanibel, Florida.
I Need a Hug! (Honor Book) by first graders of Clara Barton Elementary School, Bordentown, New Jersey.

1990: *There's a Cricket in the Library* by fifth graders of McKee Elementary School, Oakdale, Pennsylvania.

1989: *The Farmer's Huge Carrot* by kindergartners of Henry O. Tanner Kindergarten School, West Columbia, Texas.

1988: *Friendship for Three* by fourth graders of Samuel S. Nixon Elementary School, Carnegie, Pennsylvania.

1987: *A Caterpillar's Wish* by first graders of Alexander R. Shepherd School, Washington, D.C.

1986: *Looking for a Rainbow* by kindergartners of Paul Mort Elementary School, Tampa, Florida.